MY FATHER SHOULD DIE IN WINTER

MY FATHER SHOULD DIE IN WINTER
Barry Marks

BRICK ROAD
POETRY PRESS

Brick Road Poetry Press
www.brickroadpoetrypress.com

Asher, 1926 – 2017

Leah, 1990 – 2007

Noah, 2007 -

Table of Contents

My Father Should Die in Winter

Not because winter kills
all things that cast a shadow.
Not because its wind

so wounds the trees
they stand naked
in their sorrow.

Neither because the world loses color
as he loses words, nor because
home is pared to the face

of a fireplace, the way rooms
shrink after winter storms
to circles made of candlelight.

My father and I
sit before the television
and watch each other.
I try to avoid what his eyes

ask of my hands.
I have spent a lifetime
believing a word would warm
the air between us.

Now I know better.
I know my best words are
like leaves too strong
to fall until the last wind.

They will be trapped
all winter
in prisons of ice,
staring at the sun.

Buck Creek   Winter, 1937

It was a wolf winter, their bellies so empty they felt their bones sag and feared they'd cave like the swaybacked barn that ramshackled apart at first snow. So the father handed his eldest his old thirty-ought six and the boy his warmest woolen scarf, then shouldered the new rifle as they left before dawn. The snow was painfully bright even at that hour and made that sound, somewhere between a crunch and a groan, only snow can call out when the foot tamps it down. They crossed the tobacco field, into the woods. By first light they were over the ridge and were it not known land, their land, they would be lost without road or rock to mark their way, just trees lined up like some silent army waiting for a forgotten command. The boy kept lagging behind, but the father was patient and said nothing as he slowed or even backtracked. The first born never even looked back, just kept walking and straining to find a track, scat, a gnawed bit of bark, anything that might mean game or danger. It was as the father was catching up, saying they had to slow down, that they heard the boy cry out and the growl of the awakened bear, moving faster than such a burdensome mass of fat and fur should be able as it barreled up the slope with the boy in its sights and the father swung around, yanking the new rifle to his shoulder but the shot went wide and the bear was on the boy before he could get off a second to save his only son. That was when his daughter raised the old rifle and put a round square in the bear's heart, the bullet passing so close to the boy that his ear hurt from the rush of cold air. And when they pulled the bear's dead bulk off the boy he was crying and clung to his father like he hadn't since he learned to walk. And the eldest, pushing a lock of her blonde hair over her ear, leaned over the bear wondering if its winter-starved haunches would yield enough meat to last them.

Castello di Postignano

Every summer your great grandma
made us climb halfway into
the Carolina blue sky
to look for blueberries on *Satulah*,
a Cherokee word I think means
*mountain where everything
grows but blueberries.*

She found berries there once.
So she kept trying, defying logic
and the definition of insanity.

Which might explain why
I'm at another writing retreat,
this time at a castle, a real one,
learning again to show, not tell.
It's the last night,
my bags are by the door.
I'm climbing the tower
to look for constellations,
though we both know I do better
stringing lights between fireflies.
I'm trying to reach you one more time.

I want to tell you how
the workmen here found frescoes
behind a wall that collapsed,
a sort of architectural *pentimento.*
I want to show you how
the colors never faded.

I want you to know I will look
for you in the stars as I look for
you at the stars.
I will write you
though I cannot write you
back into this world.

In the beginning, shards of light
spilled across the night sky,
some too beautiful to become stars.
I will look for them behind the darkness.

Buck Creek   Spring, 1938

Everything about it was wrong and there was no way a father could make it right. Not this time. It was spring, when things are supposed to spring to life. The fields and woods and bellies full of life. Full the way he was when he first married her mother, those nights when he took her to bed so full he thought he would burst at the seams until he spilled out into her. Like the way her belly filled with the two they brought into the world, filled out and stretched until he thought he could see their faces pressing against his wife's taut flesh, straining to get out, more like a bird fighting its way out of the shell than a human baby. Especially his daughter, his firstborn, so full of life and so fed up with waiting she kicked and rolled until his wife swore she was either twins or some sort of Goliath and then there she was, shockingly frail, shockingly female, but her eyes wide open, looking about the room although the midwife, laughing, swore newborns couldn't see anything. Full of life from that first moment, and ready to take it on. Not like the boy, cut from his mother because he wasn't ready to be born and then screaming, eyes shut, red-faced, never quite ready to face up to life. Book-loving. Gentle. More like his mother and loved for it. He was the one you feared would fall through the ice in March, step onto a satinback in August, inhale the poison breath of a witch virus or the chill of some newly-named haint resistant to poultice and pill. He was the one to worry over, the one to pray for, not the daughter. And it was the daughter who, that last cold night of the bad winter, took a chill and stopped living. The preacher told him the law said she had to be laid to rest in a proper place and that the churchyard was best for all, but the father knew better. She was not going into some hole the hired man would dig in the manicured grass behind that very church she schemed and plotted to avoid each Sunday, her excuses becoming so creative even her mother laughed and gave in. These were the woods she loved, and if her father's hands could not build her a home or raise a barn for her and the husband she would never know, he could right well make her a place in the earth. And he did. Walking back, his chest feeling at once too heavy to bear and hollow as a long-dead chestnut, he looked to the sky and wondered how long before its empty blue mouth inhaled the part of him he struggled to carry home.

Let Me Show You What Every Boy Should Know about His Gran'pa's Timex

It really should be gold, shouldn't it?
A gold pocket watch with a hunter's case,
a photo of your grandmother inside.
Then again, this wristwatch is more appropriate.
Gran'pa isn't the pocketwatch sort.

Takes a lickin'
and keeps on tickin'
That was the commercial when I was your age.
They'd strap one to a diver and show him
doing a swan dive off a cliff.

When he climbed out
they'd focus the camera
on the watch,
dripping wet but
still be ticking the seconds.

Tick.
Tick.
Tick.
Have you ever heard a wristwatch
make that sound?

Let's get the glass off first.
It's called a *crystal*.
I don't know, maybe once
they were made of crystal.
This little crack means it must be replaced.

Look through it. It's clear
and a mirror at the same time.
When the light is right, you can see me,
with your reflection alongside.
I saw Gran'Pa that way.

Look it in the face.
Don't touch the hands.
Naked, they are so frail.
Now let's flip it over
and take a look.

This back panel is so old it's worn smooth.
Sweat, the body's acid, does that.
Never said anything anyway, except maybe
that it was waterproof, shockproof and
made in someplace they buy time low, sell high.

There, that's the *mainspring*.
Main.
Spring.
This is what brings the watch to life.
It's the driving force.

If the mainspring is strong,
a watch like this will last long.
Long after it's out of style, after
it's a creaky old thing
with a cracked crystal.

And next to it, the *going train*.
It's a *gear train*.
Trains move things, right?
The going train transmits the mainspring's force

but that would be worthless without this.

The *balance wheel.*
Everything stays uniform because of
the balance wheel.
A second lasts a second,
a minute lasts 60 seconds.

You can be sure of it.
Every time.
Reliable.
Certain.
Balanced.

And all of it would be useless
were it not for this.
Know what it is?
The *escapement.*
The escapement allows the energy

to get out of the box of springs
and wheels and gears
to move those frail little hands.
It doesn't matter how good the mechanism,
if all that good stuff stays inside.

Let's put it all back together and take it
to show Gran'pa when we visit.
Maybe he will say something.
Maybe he will smile.
He would have liked to know you better.
but time sort of caught up with him.

One more thing. You'll see all kinds of stuff
on watches: timers and time zones, date-keepers
and every kind of upgrade they
can imagine to make a simple watch
something more.

Just remember one thing.
In watch circles
those are called *complications*.
This will mean more to you
when I am winding down.

Buck Creek   Summer, 1938

His mama's aunt went silent back in '15, meaning he only had vague recollections of her voice. She never said much and none of it happy. His more recent memories were of something dried, a husk sewn into a rocking chair, a scarecrow whose hollow eyes fixed on the road but never registered any change no matter what drove by. To him, she was the witch out of his meemaw's tales, only harmless. Words, he decided long ago, were the necessary elements of spells. Without them, a witch was just an old woman, her evil magic roiling in her skull and doing no one else any harm. It was different with the girl from Atlanta. Her rich pappy went off the Franklin road one night, probably drunk, and the Ford dropped about a thousand feet toward the *Callusaja*. It stopped halfway down, stacked vertical against a tree, nose down, the old man's neck broke, his wife thrown out and crushed against a boulder at the bottom of the gorge, and the girl child, trapped in the back seat, her leg bent backwards like a tree limb too green to break off. Three days and two nights she sat in that car, screaming, everyone said, staring down through the shattered windshield. Somehow they got her out but the effort loosed the tree's hold so the car and her father joined her mother's corpse the rest of the way down. They say she looked at the car as it slipped away and then her face went blank. Whatever magic might live in a young girl's heart turned to ice that day. She didn't sit on a porch like his aunt, but in a bed in some private hospital. There were others he knew of. A soldier, his face shot away and apparently his words with it. A young mother who barely survived childbirth but whose heart stopped just long enough to silence her forever. All of them, he imagined, were listening to this storm as it roared up the valley on its way to Cashiers and beyond. Summer storms, wind and rain, sometimes hail, challenged the best-framed barns and houses. Lightning seared light into bedrooms and thunder chased children and their mothers alike under beds as hounds and cats put off their hatred to share the real estate under porches. Folks say they saw haints, demons and dark women flying across the skies, driving storm clouds before them. Random possessions, from porch swings to wheelbarrows, were known to fly through windows and drop through roofs. He leaned his shoulder against the front door and staggered out onto the porch. His wife, down in the churchyard would be shivering the way she always did when the thunder shook her bones. He squinted out into the storm and tried not to think about how she would burrow beneath his arm and fall asleep before the chaos let up, how it made him feel invulnerable and sure his joy would last forever, that this was what God intended and all of heaven swore to him it would continue as long as he was true to her. Straining to stand against the force, he understood why so many went silent. He felt the power of speech tease his brain before being wafted away, just as it had every day for these three years. He threw a sigh into the storm as he turned and then was pushed along on his way back into the dark house where the boy would be huddled in terror, waiting for him to offer comfort and promises he did not have to give. How could he say something magical that would make the storm go away, make it all good again, when he knew the wind spoke his heart better than any words his mind could conjure?

The Sargasso Sea and the Sunset Canal

When your aunt and I would lean over
the bridge above Sunset Canal,
where older boys gigged mullet
and the occasional manatee
would glide by looking like something
made of milk in the green water, itself
dangerous with barracuda or worse.
We would drop pennies
and shudder to think
how it must be for them.

Then we would spit over the railing
to touch the surface
and probe what lurked beneath.

It was as if the things we dropped
into the water's maw no longer existed,
but of course they continued,
even the saliva as it lost its borders
was still there in the water,
still real to itself,
real as the Sargasso,
because everything is as real
as it is remembered.

Buck Creek   Fall, 1938

This was the boy's favorite season. Somehow, he thought of autumn as spicy. Brown like cinnamon, red like the cinnamon candy he got on his birthday three years ago, the last one with his mother. So the last one he would ever have. Why did good memories make you sad? Why did the things that made them never stay? Like the leaves, they turned red and gold and then died. It was so true it hurt his chest to think about it. So he didn't. He was learning to not think about some things. Many things. He tried to tell his father he liked fall once, and the old man almost smiled, his tobacco breath, brown spicy breath, let out a single "yes." It was a good day. He didn't like winter. Winter was a giant black bear like the one he had to not think about. He was cold and afraid all winter long. And summer was worse, at least much of the time. Things came out and crawled, waiting for him. The big rattlesnakes, satinbacks, were scariest to most folks. Silent copperheads were harder to avoid, although their poison wasn't near as deadly. Full grown copperheads often gave a dry bite, just a warning. The babies were worse, born mean and unable, or just unwilling, to hold back their venom. He was most afraid of the water snakes. He no longer even swam in Mirror Lake or down in the Callusaja. The slow water by the lake shores or river bends were the home of black, vicious water moccasins, their cottony mouths the stuff of many of his nightmares. Summer meant water moccasins. And storms. Bone-rattling thunder and rain drumming the tin roof like a crazy bear with steel claws, trying to get in. *That* bear, the one he smelled every time he was afraid. Spring was nice, for a time. There was a day he woke up and everything had exploded into color, azaleas and wisteria in the valleys where the sun was freest to run her hand lightly over the soil. There would be mountain laurel and rhododendron higher up the mountains and, when he walked the forest, he would see tiny red and blue and purple flowers as sudden as lightning, strewn about wherever the leaves parted enough to let the sun reach in. The sun always tried to reach in. But come spring, his silent father's face darkened even further and closed even more and he didn't even answer the boy's questions but stared ahead as if only a fool would ask, so he stopped.

17

Pelican Bay

Each goddam pelican has his piling
three—four—six feet above the tide.
Everything has to have its own damned turf,
boundaries, good fences, whatever the hell.
So this one circles around into the wind
(of course they're all facing into the wind
life is facing the goddam wind)
so this bastard comes up behind one squatter
and then drops down and the other guy
rears up and starts flapping, too, they both
start squawking something godawful with one
just above the other and then the first one,
the new guy, heads back to the sky and does
another slow circle before he gives up
and heads off to the next row of pilings
where I guess he sees a vacancy but
what do you think the other guy, the squatter, does?
He spreads out and launches off his spot, dropping
three-four feet so you hear a slap, slap,
and you think it's his wings slapping the water
but it's his feet pushing against the water to bounce
his ass up so the wings can work (when your wings
hit the water you're done for, after all)
and slap-slap-slap he's up a foot above the waves,
shooting off to find a fish or something
or because he's bored or bird-horny
or whatever the hell gives Pelicans an itch,
while the others sit there through the whole show
bills tucked in, about as interested as
the sky or the Spanish moss on the shore trees

or the sides of the dozen RVs next door
where a door slams and someone calls
Stu? but no one says *Yeh?* And the waves
slap the shore and then there's a car
and everyone is living on his own little spot
in his own little house in his own little body
except you, of course, and it made me think
I'd like to show you tonight, that's all.

Buck Creek   Spring, 1940

When night departed it left shadows, doubling the layers of mountains that climbed row-on-row into the sky and dared the boy to cast his eyes all the way into the clear color of morning. In the cold newborn air, he would perch on Sunrise Rock and dangle his feet perilously over death. Each time, Horse Cove below whispered him forward, to test the air. The voices of a dozen confederate mounts sacrificed to feed Hunt's cavalry and forestall the men's defeat called to him to step away. Often he would say "No" loudly enough to stir a few birds. Soon the sun would chase him back to his father's house where his chores awaited. Then to the schoolhouse where Mrs. Talley would be kind to him because he knew the answers and had read the lesson and because, for a time, the other boys teased him and asked what the bear did when it gave him that big hug. They would take turns sneaking up behind him and growling, but after a short while, he no longer flinched. He learned not to hear.

Myself and Others

We are fine, really,
although some days we lie in bed
an extra hour and it takes a third
cup of coffee to set the world
back on its axis.

We do not avoid sad things
as you might expect;
we remember the words to songs,
the names of pets and people;
we find new meanings in them all.

We turn from fantasy because it opens
doors; no one is more grounded,
no one less trusting of hope.

We exist with our existence;
we know what is here and cope.
We cope very well, thank you,
with what is here and what is not:

how stars are unseen in daylight
and shadows in night;
how the edge of the world waits
a step beyond our vision;
how suicide sits beside us at breakfast
and dares us to pass
the butter, the knife.

Buck Creek   Fall, 1944

The morning they buried his father was not as cold as it should have been. The boy wanted their breath to show, the last spring frost to bore itself into each of them, family, friends, earth, sky and whatever ghosts wandered this place. Bore in like a wasp into a caterpillar, leaving a cold that would consume them in time. He wanted this moment to be frozen into his memory always. Not enough. It was not enough.

So this was God. Not enough. Whatever the preacher said about a better place, it was up to people to make things right. To do what need be done. Sarah saving him from the bear was not God's doing, it was Sarah's. Losing Sarah was not God's fault. It was because there was not the right medicine. That was why he had to fight to remember her face, her smell, the soft feel of her finger drawing shapes on his arm to help him throw off his fears and sleep. "Light as a pencil," Sarah would say in the language only they spoke.

His mother, his father, Sarah, the squirrels and deer they ate. The bear. The chestnuts, all ghost grey and hollow, standing like a glimpse of the future amid the healthy, green and growing forest. Mrs. Talley told his class the mountains were among the oldest in the world, worn down by wind and rain. They were dying beneath his feet.

That was all the God there was and all he wanted.

Sarah always did what need be done. She never wasted time telling him that she loved him. Even after that day, when he wet the bed but his father said it was high time he slept on his own anyway, even when she came to his bed some nights and lay down with him until he was asleep, she never wasted a minute's breath on anything that did not need be said. He would do what need be done from now on.

No more wasting time thinking about things. No more playing with words, the words that kept him up at night, the words that kept hiding from him, calling to him and teasing him. No more of that. He would study. He would work. He would go to school and become a doctor. He would live because that is what need be done.

To the Third and Fourth Generation

Exodus 20:5

1. Man Caves in the Promised Land

men hide

they hide in women's eyes
they hide in the eyes of other men
men hide in helmets
in Ferraris and Fords
and latex
and the coach car on the way to work
the lounge car on the way home
and Club Cars on Saturday afternoons

men hide
   in football that is or isn't soccer
   and in sweat
   in music and metaphor
   in their names   in their children
   in public office   in private space
   in designer clothes   in boxer shorts
   in animal skins   in their own flesh
   in stoicism   and in rage
   in emotions they do not feel
   behind Glocks and Uzis and AK-47s
   in first class   on barstools
     in the Swimsuit Issue

men hide in trenches and go over the top when they must

and then they take the last express home

2. Men Go Over the Top

men love their mothers
and kill their fathers with swords
sometimes in myth
and other times in rage
or insanity

men kiss their mothers without shame
and their fathers goodbye at the station

when they grow up real men take their own trains
to their own trenches

3. Doc Holliday, Dentist with a .44

Doc Holliday was dying
so he became a gunfighter
to kill time
he was a real man
until he rode the Union Pacific
to a Colorado sanitarium where
being childless
he was swallowed by legend
and lost to history

men die
they are killed by cape buffalo
who run every which way
and refuse to go gently onto the man cave wall
men are killed by *fer de lance* and black mamba
staphylococcous
and medical malpractice
random things
subtle things
blackwater things they do not want to name
men are killed by crocodiles lurking beneath the Nile
they refuse to admit that they are killed by trains
because trains run on tracks following the lights on their faces
on time   in time   of time
trains are timely   when they stay on track
they only stop when they reach the end of the line
men pretend that they love trains
men who have seen the light
sneer at men who are in the dark
even if the light only reaches enlightened men
at the end of the tunnel or

27

in Einstein's railcar
rushing to a black hole men
pretend not to understand
as they boldly sink into the Nile

5. The Denial of Ham

men see their fathers naked
when they are children
and when they change their fathers' diapers

men see their fathers in their hands
men see their fathers in their hands
men hide their eyes behind their hands
the way their fathers did
and then drop their hands to delight their sons
the way their fathers did
they are there and then they are not
and they are again
men kiss their fathers goodbye

brave men do not expose themselves
brave men do not need to kiss their fathers goodbye
but they do

6. Why Men Expose Themselves

…exhibitionism is a crude attempt to alleviate overwhelming fears of castration.
—Aggrawal, *Forensic and Medico-Legal Aspects of Sexual Crimes*

Butch and Sundance jump from a moving train
because in the movies
men jump from moving trains

real men jump from the corner office
and from 135,908 feet to set a new record
because they have parachutes

men who fear heights do not lean off high buildings
or look up from the sidewalk at high buildings
men who fear heights stay off high buildings
not because they are afraid they will fall
because they are afraid they will jump

7. Real Men Leave the Tracks

my father gets up from his comfortable seat
in the best car on the train
he stoops beneath the weight
of the 21 grams that are his soul
he walks through the dining car
he smiles at the woman sitting by the window
he goes through a door to stand between the cars
he opens another door and leans out
he looks behind
forward
down
he straightens his back
then steps into the air
and is lost to memory

Buck Creek   Winter, 1946

A man rises from his bed, his blanket wrapped about his shoulders. He walks to a window and stares into the night. Across the landscape, the snow is charged with moonlight. Burly winter wind growls behind the trees but the way to the barn is still. From the woods, the snow is dotted with furtive tracks that end in a roil of snow.

The man turns from the window, places a log on the fire and watches sparks float as the wood hisses and cracks. If the house burns, all that will be left will be this fireplace and the brick chimney, coal-black inside, its open head thrusting for the sky. He whispers that fire sleeps in wood as death sleeps in bone and rage behind the eyes of every good man..

The man lowers his eyes, and returns to the bed, pulls the covers to his chin, and listens to the fire, the wind, the night, a choice with which he will live the rest of his life.

No Parachute

*The Hun I am fighting may be calling on Him too…How can I call on God to help
me shoot down a man in flames?*
—Arthur Gould Lee, Air Vice-Marshal, Royal Air Force, *No Parachute:
A Classic Account of War in the Air in WWI*

You know this place.
Gray-stubbled men surround an oil drum fire,
most in tattered charnel-house coats,
blowing into their hands and doing
that dance men do when the cold
sinks its spurs in their bones.
That one there, closest the fire, the one not
dancing but glowering in his chair, empty
pants legs clipped shut, green jacket
whispering a faded name.
That one calls to you.
You know what he is going to say, don't you?
How if his first prayer were answered,
the bastards would know because his legs would grow back
and he would kick their sorry asses from
Kabul to Kingdom Come,
then get to work on their children.
And what can you say?
It is not the bare concrete chill of November
that makes you shudder as you walk from the fire.
It is what you know. What you always knew.
You walk past St. Stephen's and Beth Israel, First
Calvary and the library and the market and the graveyard.
You raise up your grief and your voice but you hear
only shivering stars in a barren sky:
What God do you fear
more than the One who will not

33

answer the prayers of the righteous?

The Man in the Glass Booth

Music is made by a man in a glass booth.

Clark Kent steps out of a glass booth
and is Superman.
There was a man in a glass booth
who thought he was a superman, entitled
to kill lesser men and women.
When the floor fell away,
in his last heartbeat,
he flew.

Music is made by a man in a glass booth.
Everyone can see as he drinks,
as he smokes,
as he shoots up,
as he fumbles with his fly.
Everyone can see him and they ask,
Is that really where the music comes from?

This man in this glass booth
sees the woman seeing him.
When the light is right he can see
himself next to her.
It is a property of glass
to be at once reflective and transparent,
like the eyes of a lover.
The eyes of a lover are glass.
The eyes of a lover create rainbows
and walls.

Sometimes the man
in the glass booth lets people
throw stones at him.
No one gets the joke.

If you visit his house you will see
all is in order:
the bed is made,
the floors are clean,
the dishes are stacked.
The man in the glass booth is all right.

But when he watches a documentary
about the monkfish,
the man in the glass booth
eyes his sofa nervously.

There is a door in the glass booth.
Does it have a handle on the inside
or on the outside?
Come inside and tell me.

Buck Creek   Summer, 1966

We stop for lunch in Dublin, Georgia, off 441 (the "Uncle Remus Route"). A fat black lady puts a plate of collards and black-eyed peas in front of Dad and I almost choke on the smell but his eyes light up like it's Christmas, the way Sarah and I haven't seen since this time last year.

We call him the Bear, and cringe when mom sends him in to kiss us goodnight and his face is all rough with black stubble. And he's a bear because he is always grouchy except in July when we go up to the mountains and he forgets to be angry.

We know he's going to change when he starts to hum just below Valdosta. If we say we're thirsty, he sings

> *All day I've faced the barren wastes without the taste of water. Coo-ool*
> *wat-ter.*
> *Oh, Dan and I with throats burned dry and souls that cry fo-or water,*
> *coo-ool,*
> *cle-ar wat-ter.*

If I try to sing along he tells me I inherited my mother's voice. And of course he doesn't stop, even if we say we need to use the bathroom, but he smiles that smile like we're in on the joke, too. Until mom tells him we have to stop and then he growls a little. But just a little.

The Girl

who loved Night left a flower by her window each morning. She closed the curtains as she slept, opening them only at dusk to let in the dark. And Night came to her each day like a cat roused from hiding by its mistress's song. Night shone through the girl's stained glass love, painting colors it never thought to own across the floor. One day, as her father slept, the girl who loved Night rose from her bed and followed Death's burning bell to find Night waiting. And the old man, sifting the remains of their home in his grief, found Night's shadow etched in smoke on her bed but did not recognize his old love until he noticed the charred and fragrant rose lying between his daughter's bed and the open window.

The Man

who is loved by Death dances between Earth and Moon, his body making a place for itself in the air. He brandishes Life's terrible gift as he levers himself out of bed each morning by the simple tool of his will. For all his fifty-odd years, he has carried the weight of his father's heaven, to no end. And Death watches, hiding behind the shadow of a bedpost. As the man who is loved by Death feels his guttering hours flicker, he dances faster, reaching to touch and taste his memories with the peculiar synesthesia of love. And still Death sings, calling him to dance with *her*. Each night the man who is loved by Death has called his daughter's name from his sleep and thought to hear it echo as he woke. But today, he hears only the answer of a morning owl. And for the first time in a very long time, Death smiles her patient smile.

Exit Strategy

It is the worst pain in the world
and/ but/ because
it doesn't hurt a bit.
This house has seven rooms
not counting the bathrooms.

He is in each one, except the couple
she is in (or so the doctor assures me),
usually frowning, sometimes angry,
sometimes very.

I can avoid his/her eyes
sometimes
if I dive into a book or the t.v. but
either is a shallow pool.

Most of the time we have to talk
because/ although/ whether or not
we hate to talk. The neighbors
must be concerned.

Things can get heated.
How to find a door that opens out?
Front/ back/ any door?
How to say at last
enough/ shut up/ I love you?

Let yourself.

In Other Words

God has given you one face and you make yourself another
—Shakespeare, *Hamlet* III, 1

Other days he was fine.
He watched the Dolphins lose.
He ate what they fed him
and thought of pecan pie.
He let his songs play in his head
and forgot what the words meant.
He did not think about walking.

1952.
Walking to work every night.
There were two hours before the late shift
at Mass General, his wife back
home with their son. The gray winter
was no place for a Miami girl,
or a Georgia boy, not that he let it matter.

Coffee and cigarette smoke.
The club was a block from the ER.
Johnny Moore's Three Blazers
      How Deep is the Ocean,
Charles Brown
      Homesick Blues,
Josh White
      St. James Infirmary Blues,

The King Cole Trio
      Stardust,
      September Song,
      Fly Me to the Moon,
      A Nightingale Sang in Berkley Square.

41

He sang along until the songs were his.

Nat King Cole and George Shearing
came with the Stromberg-Carlson in 1963,
along with *Sinatra's Greatest, Ferrante & Teicher,*
and *Jerry Colonna Entertains at Your Party.*
He bought a dozen more albums, now boxed
along with everything else.

Boston. Buck Creek.
Places where the leaves changed and
each day was not like the last,
not like the next. In Miami,
the sun shined every day
like a promise to a child,
but it rained every afternoon.

There was something he wanted to say.

When I fall in love it will be forever
or I'll never fall in love
In a restless world like this is
love is ended before it's begun,
and too many moonlight kisses
seem to cool in the warmth of the sun...

On the good days,
he sang to himself
and forgot the sun's promise
not to let this day ever come.

The air sang in the vents like
a nameless memory.
There was something he wanted to say.

Something to explain, to take back,
to tell them about a café in 1952,
but the words faded into melody.
And the sun shined like a broken promise.

Today She Would Have Been 30

The plural of *myriad* is *myriads*,
which I find problematic.

If *myriad* means an indefinitely,
indefinably large number of things,
an innumerable number,
then *myriads* can only exist if we
group such things together
into individual, identifiable myriads,
each of which would, by definition,
contain an indefinite, innumerable
number of the things in question.

Those things, being indefinite in number,
would bleed outside the boundaries
of their respective myriads
and into other myriads,
creating a single, indefinitely large
myriad.

It is like how the Hebrews first described
Hashem (meaning *The Name*, because
God's name was unpronounceable and itself
too great to be known by just anyone) as
One,
meaning not only singular,
but too vast to be contained and leaving
no room for any other.

Isn't this why we never say *universes*
or *eternities* and only poetically speak of

the heavens (*heavens* being confusingly used
to mean the one place in some texts);
the way I grow dizzy looking for you
in the sky that goes on forever
and only ends where we call it *space*.

Think of the difference between *space*
and s*paces*, *room* and *rooms*,
time and *times*,
night and day and
nights and days;

wait a second means
an indefinite pause, never one sixtieth of a minute,
but *wait thirty seconds* leaves us counting
one one thousand, two one thousand, three one thousand
four...
five...
six...
seven...
eight...
nine...
ten...
all the enumerated seconds,
leading to all the minutes,
hours, days,
years,
decades
and *millennia* more indefinite,
more unending than a specified
number of thousand-year intervals?

Don't you see how the plural
makes things specific, countable,
harder to bear? Don't you see
how this explains
the myriad ways truth
is true in all the world
and love, grief and hope
fill all the room in the heart
and all the space there is.
Everywhere.

Buck Creek   Winter, 2017

The boy closed his eyes and it all went away at last. The overbright light. The chemical smells. The sound of the heart machine, the lung machine, the blood machine and the absence of human sound. As a lesser dream masquerades as an hour or a day, so his last dream defied time. He was riding a bear, the bear, across a landscape of glowing, unblemished snow. The bear lumbered on over drifts and between hills, leaping across valleys and finally following the snowy path up into the clouds. Ahead, he saw his father take off the oil-stained ball cap the boy hadn't thought of in years. His mother stood by the door of their home, her face flecked with flour. In the distance he heard his sister taunting him for being late for supper. The bear stopped to let him down, and became the brother he never had, tagging along behind him, trying to match his steps. It was winter and then it was spring and it was summer and then, for a very long time, it was fall. The seasons and the years rolled on and there was a fire in the fireplace and Jimmy Rogers on the radio and all the smells and tastes and thoughts that he had forgotten. Things he sacrificed to the needs of being a man. And, like any dream, what others would say lasted only an instant to the boy was eternity.

About the Author

Barry Marks is a Birmingham attorney. His most recent book, *Dividing By Zero*, combines poetry, narrative and fiction to tell the story of the damage caused by a writer's self-possession. *Possible Crocodiles*, his first book, was named 2010 Book of the Year by the Alabama State Poetry Society. *Sounding*, his second book, was a finalist for the Eric Hoffer Award for Independent Publishers. Barry's most recent project is a pair of poetry/music collaborations with Professor Alan Goldspiel of the University of Montevallo. The first, *Sometimes Y*, has been performed at music conferences and universities around the country, and the second, tentatively entitled *and Sons*, is a companion to this book. Barry was Alabama's Poet of the Year for 1999 and twice President of the Alabama State Poetry Society.

Acknowledgments

Earlier versions of the following poems have been or will be published in the journals listed opposite their names.

"My Father Should Die in Winter" *Birmingham Poetry Review*
"Castello di Postignano" *Birmingham Arts Journal*

Excerpts from certain of the poems in this book have been used to create *and Sons*, a musical and poetry production with Professor Alan Goldspiel of the University of Montevallo. The recorded version of that production is expected to be available in early 2022.

Author's Note

Many of the poems in this book, and especially the "Buck Creek" poems were written to be read aloud.

Our Mission

BRICK ROAD

POETRY PRESS

The mission of Brick Road Poetry Press is to publish and promote poetry that entertains, amuses, edifies, and surprises a wide audience of appreciative readers. We are not qualified to judge who deserves to be published, so we concentrate on publishing what we enjoy. Our preference is for poetry geared toward dramatizing the human experience in language rich with sensory image and metaphor, recognizing that poetry can be, at one and the same time, both familiar as the perspiration of daily labor and as outrageous as a carnival sideshow.

Available from Brick Road Poetry Press

BRICK ROAD

POETRY PRESS

www.brickroadpoetrypress.com

The Word in Edgewise by Sean M. Conrey

Household Inventory by Connie Jordan Green

Practice by Richard M. Berlin

A Meal Like That by Albert Garcia

Cracker Sonnets by Amy Wright

Things Seen by Joseph Stanton

Battle Sleep by Shannon Tate Jonas

Lauren Bacall Shares a Limousine by Susan J. Erickson

Ambushing Water by Danielle Hanson

Having and Keeping by David Watts

Assisted Living by Erin Murphy

Credo by Steve McDonald

The Deer's Bandanna by David Oates

Creation Story by Steven Owen Shields

Touring the Shadow Factory by Gary Stein

American Mythology by Raphael Kosek

Waxing the Dents by Daniel Edward Moore

Speaking Parts by Beth Ruscio

Also Available from Brick Road Poetry Press

www.brickroadpoetrypress.com

Dancing on the Rim by Clela Reed

Possible Crocodiles by Barry Marks

Pain Diary by Joseph D. Reich

Otherness by M. Ayodele Heath

Drunken Robins by David Oates

Damnatio Memoriae by Michael Meyerhofer

Lotus Buffet by Rupert Fike

The Melancholy MBA by Richard Donnelly

Two-Star General by Grey Held

Chosen by Toni Thomas

Etch and Blur by Jamie Thomas

Water-Rites by Ann E. Michael

Bad Behavior by Michael Steffen

Tracing the Lines by Susanna Lang

Rising to the Rim by Carol Tyx

Treading Water with God by Veronica Badowski

Rich Man's Son by Ron Self

Just Drive by Robert Cooperman

The Alp at the End of My Street by Gary Leising

About the Prize

BRICK ROAD

POETRY PRESS

The Brick Road Poetry Prize, established in 2010, is awarded annually for the best book-length poetry manuscript. Entries are accepted August 1st through November 1st. The winner receives $1000 and publication. For details on our preferences and the complete submission guidelines, please visit our website at www.brickroadpoetrypress.com.

Winners of the Brick Road Poetry Prize

2019

Return of the Naked Man by Robert Tremmel

2018

Speaking Parts by Beth Ruscio

2017

Touring the Shadow Factory by Gary Stein

2016

Assisted Living by Erin Murphy

2015

Lauren Bacall Shares a Limousine by Susan J. Erickson

2014

Battle Sleep by Shannon Tate Jonas

2013

Household Inventory by Connie Jordan Green

2012

The Alp at the End of My Street by Gary Leising

2011

Bad Behavior by Michael Steffen

2010

Damnatio Memoriae by Michael Meyerhofer